THE ULTIMATE HURDLER
HURRICANE
FLY

THE ULTIMATE HURDLER

HURRICANE
FLY

Edited by ANDREW PENNINGTON

RACING POST

First published in Great Britain in 2015 byRacing Post Books
27 Kingfisher Court, Hambridge Road, Newbury, Berkshire, RG14 5SJ

10 9 8 7 6 5 4 3 2 1

A catalogue record for this book is available from the British Library.

ISBN 978-1-910498-69-9

Cover design by Jay Vincent and Nathan Bines
Text designed by J Schwartz & Co.
Printed and bound in Italy by L.E.G.O. S.p.A

www.racingpost.com/shop

CONTENTS

FOREWORD

MY FATHER once told me I can watch the videos of Dawn Run, look at the pictures and read the books but I'll never truly understand what it meant at that exact moment in time because nobody then knew what would happen. You didn't have the build-up, the doubts and the unanswered questions, he said. Nobody expected, as we do now watching the replays, that the mare would get up.

The emotions that watching Hurricane Fly race has given us is what epitomises why we race horses. The excitement of what might be from his early victories being baked in the pressure before his first Champion Hurdle. The bitter disappointment and disbelief of his first Champion Hurdle defeat when he was the Irish banker.

That sick feeling in the bottom of my stomach the next year when Ruby was shovelling coal at halfway suddenly turning to a roar in the back of my throat as Fly clawed his way to the front and toughed it out up that long and unforgiving hill to reclaim the crown that he had lost.

I remember the sense of dread when the new wonderkid, Our Conor, loomed up in bright yellow with Danny motionless and Ruby fiercely at work and even landed in front of Fly at the back of the last. How Fly wordlessly snarled 'Thou Shalt Not Pass', and the sheer pride as he strained every possible sinew he had and fought tooth and nail to victory. And then thinking this is the beginning of the end when Jezki bested him in Punchestown after beating him at Cheltenham too.

I can't forget the 'this could be the final time' feeling every time he won that last season. The ecstatic happiness as he fended off the reigning champion Jezki not once, not twice but three times in battle. The rush of pure adrenalin and excitement as himself and Jezki thundered furiously

towards the last, McCoy vs Walsh a forgotten side battle. The wall of sound that greeted him in Leopardstown after that final win is something etched into my memory forever.

If watching him rage against the dying of the light with his head down, his ears back and that fire in his eye never made the hair above the tip of your spine stand bolt upright and your heart race faster, never made you jump in the air in delight and punch the air in celebration, never made you clench your fist in willing him on and roar out the war cry that was 'Come on The FLY!' or never made you simply just nod your head in appreciation that here was a horse out of the ordinary, a horse that was worth actually going to the races to see him run, then perhaps my friend you are in the wrong sport or maybe you were forged in a place elsewhere than the rest of us.

What days were you there?

Do you remember it all?

You can become a champion on a day, or perhaps in a season. You can win the title champion. But you have to earn greatness. Hurricane Fly earned his greatness over seven seasons with class, determination and bravery beyond the call of duty.

Fly has given us moments in time that we'll never forget and while I'm gutted I'll never again get to roar at the top of my lungs 'Come on The Fly', in celebration or desperation, boy am I glad I got to shout it in the first place. And maybe one day I'll try explain to a child what exactly it meant at the time, just like my father did about Dawn Run to me.

The Hurricane Fly story has come to an end and I feel lucky to have watched it unfold before me.

Farewell The Fly.

Paddy Mullins

PATRICK MULLINS
September 2015

CAREER OVERVIEW

Alan Sweetman looks back on a career defined by consistency, longevity and precious talent

HURRICANE FLY exited the stage with a secure place in the pantheon of racing greats, a record-breaking hurdler associated with two masters of jump racing, trainer Willie Mullins and jockey Ruby Walsh, who rode him to 18 of 24 hurdle victories.

He accumulated a world-record 22 Grade 1 wins, surpassed the mighty Istabraq by winning the Irish Champion Hurdle five years in succession, and won the Champion Hurdle in 2011 and 2013. Although it took time for him to capture the public's imagination, he gradually endeared himself, thanks to remarkable consistency at the highest level. Ultimately he achieved a status of popularity rarely achieved, his longevity on the track a credit to Mullins and his team, and a source of immense pride for owners Rose Boyd and George Creighton.

Bred by the Agricola Del Parco and foaled on April 5, 2004, Hurricane Fly made a first public appearance when consigned from the Irish National Stud at Goffs in September 2005. With French links in his pedigree, as a son of Montjeu out of a daughter of Kenmare,

he appealed to the owner-trainer combination of Raoul Teman and Jean-Luc Pelletan, who secured him for €65,000.

Sent into training with Pelletan, he had his first race over 6f at La Teste de Buch, a provincial track in the Gironde, in July 2006, finishing second in a field of seven. Having been placed in three of his four starts at two, he opened his account over 7f at Mont-de-Marsan on his three-year-old debut in March 2007. Later that month he won a Listed race over 1m at Saint-Cloud, beating Literato, who ended the season with a Group 1 triumph in the Champion Stakes.

Graduating to Pattern company, he ran another four times in 2007, giving his best display when fourth behind subsequent Prix du Jockey Club and Prix Jean Prat winner Lawman in a 1m1f Group 3 at Chantilly.

One of many inspired purchases made on behalf of the Mullins stable in France, Hurricane Fly quickly built a strong home reputation, ensuring he was sent off at a shade of odds-on for his hurdling debut in a 22-runner maiden at Punchestown in May 2008. He won by 12 lengths under Walsh, creating a powerful impression despite a few untidy jumps, earning a return to France for a Grade 3 at Auteuil later that month. There he beat the experienced filly Grivette, who gained her revenge in the Grade 1 Prix Alain du Breil the following month, a contest in which Mullins also saddled third-placed Quevega, another future stable star.

Hurricane Fly's domestic campaign in 2008-09 saw him unbeaten in three Grade 1s, kicking off with the Royal Bond at Fairyhouse, but the season was tinged with regret as he missed the Supreme Novices' at Cheltenham, the sense of disappointment heightened when Go Native, beaten ten lengths by Hurricane Fly at Leopardstown's Christmas meeting, won the Cheltenham event.

Back in action for the Punchestown festival, Hurricane Fly relegated Go Native to fourth in beating stable companion Kempes to complete his Grade 1 hat-trick.

His first race in the senior ranks delivered an unexpected reverse when he managed only third of four runners behind Solwhit in the Morgiana Hurdle at Punchestown in November 2009, and there was more serious concern when a setback ruled him out of the big winter Grade 1s at Leopardstown and the Champion Hurdle. Against that background, Mullins viewed his rematch with Solwhit at the Punchestown festival with some trepidation, believing he was short of peak condition. However, showing great tenacity, Hurricane Fly knuckled down to edge out Solwhit by a neck.

After asserting his supremacy over Solwhit in three successive Irish Grade 1 clashes in the 2010-11 season, Hurricane Fly started favourite for the 2011 Champion Hurdle. Circumstances dictated that up until now Paul Townend had ridden him in seven of his 11 races over hurdles, but for his first Champion bid he was reunited with Walsh, who would partner him in all but one of his subsequent runs.

In an 11-strong field, Walsh was at his most unobtrusive best, getting Hurricane Run to settle well after he had threatened to boil over at the start. Jumping superbly, he got to the front perhaps a little sooner than Walsh would have wished and idled on the run-in before holding off the previous year's Neptune winner Peddlers Cross.

He was the first horse since Alderbrook in 1995 to win the race without having previously run at Cheltenham, and was a first winner at the track at the 45th attempt for his sire Montjeu.

The difficulties involved in keeping Hurricane Fly sound were exemplified by the fact he raced only twice in the 12-month period before returning to defend his crown in March 2012. However, this time he arrived at Cheltenham with stable confidence strong in the wake of a second victory in the Irish Champion Hurdle, and was sent off 4-6 favourite only to run rather flat in finishing third behind Rock On Ruby.

That unexpected defeat was the prelude to a nine-race winning sequence in Grade 1s between Punchestown in April 2012 and January 2014 when he captured the Irish Champion Hurdle for a fourth time.

He achieved all but one of eight successive wins on home soil during that period at odds-on, often with less than a handful of opponents. However, he proved equal to the greater task that confronted him in March 2013 when he gained his revenge on Rock On Ruby in the Champion Hurdle, becoming the first horse to reclaim the title since Comedy Of Errors in 1975.

By beating the previous season's brilliant Triumph winner Our Conor in the 2014 Irish Champion Hurdle, and relegating the Jessica Harrington-trained Jezki to fourth in the process, the ten-year-old Hurricane Fly did enough to make him favourite to retain his Champion Hurdle crown. However, in a race marred by the death of Our Conor he failed to show his usual zest, unable to raise his effort between the last two flights and fading into fourth behind Jezki, his junior by four years.

At the beginning of May 2014, Jezki readily confirmed the form in what was effectively a match for the Racing Post Champion Hurdle at Punchestown, and it seemed like it was the end of the line on account of him being so comprehensively usurped by a horse with youth on his side. However, such speculation proved wide of the mark when the pair clashed again in the first joust of the 2014-15 season in the Morgiana at Punchestown, when the old warrior won decisively despite a couple of uncharacteristic jumping errors.

He upheld the form in the Ryanair Hurdle at Leopardstown's Christmas meeting and returned to the track at which he was invincible to beat stable companion Arctic Fire and Jezki to record a historic fifth Irish Champion Hurdle win in January.

Conjecture about Walsh's choice of Champion Hurdle mount was one of the main themes of the season, but despite his affinity with the record-breaking 11-year-old, most informed opinion believed he could hardly ignore the claims of the undefeated Faugheen, a brilliant winner of the 2014 Neptune and unextended when landing the Christmas Hurdle at Kempton.

Walsh was always going to favour realism over sentiment, and so it was that Townend took over at Cheltenham, with Walsh on 4-5 favourite Faugheen. A new era was ushered in as Walsh gave Faugheen a no-nonsense ride for an impressive victory. Arctic Fire took second and Hurricane Fly got the better of Jezki in the battle for third, securing a clean sweep for Mullins.

At the end of April, rather than send the old boy into battle against Faugheen over 2m at Punchestown, Mullins opted for the 3m Ladbroke World Series Hurdle. Jessica Harrington had the same idea with Jezki, who got the better of this final exchange between the pair. In June he returned to France for the first time in seven years and was sent off favourite for the French Champion Hurdle over 3m1½f at Auteuil.

Never in serious contention, he finished sixth, his first time outside the first four on his 32nd and last start over hurdles.

It is up for debate as to where Hurricane Fly stands in the pecking order of Irish-trained Champion Hurdle winners. A fair assessment might be to rate him alongside another dual winner Monksfield, who operated during a golden age of hurdling, and three-time winner Istabraq, who stood head and shoulders above his contemporaries, as one of a triumvirate of greats. He passes into honourable retirement before a season when Faugheen will attempt to consolidate a status as another superb champion.

1. FRANCE

PEOPLE forget that he started in France. Hurricane Fly may have been born in the green fields of County Kildare and prepped at the Irish National Stud, but it was to France that he was sold as a foal and on the Flat there as a two- and three-year-old that he cut his racing teeth. He was, after all, bred to be a Flat horse. He was by the Arc winner and top sire Montjeu and was precocious enough to run four times as a two-year-old with two seconds and finally a third at Longchamp in September. Success in his first two races as a three-year-old was not continued through the summer but even when his hurdling career did finally get under way with Willie Mullins in Ireland it was back in France that Hurricane Fly first hit the jumping headlines.

Previous spread

AUTEUIL, 25 May 2008

Ruby Walsh crosses the line on Hurricane Fly for the biggest win of his career in France in the Grade 3 Gras Savoye Prix de Longchamp Hurdle. He ran on well to beat Grivette by a length. Trainer Willie Mullins said: 'Hurricane Fly pulled very hard but still had enough left for the end of the race. I was absolutely delighted with the way he jumped and battled.'

CLAIREFONTAINE, 14 August 2006

On his third start for trainer Jean-Luc Pelletan, the two-year-old Hurricane Fly (right) finished second behind Holocene (centre) in the Prix des Magasins Champion Tourgeville et Deauville over seven furlongs under François-Xavier Bertras.

Above

LONGCHAMP, 10 September 2006

Hurricane Fly (purple cap) hits the front but could finish only third behind winner Makaan (blue, striped cap) and Simbad (second right) in the Prix du Casino Barriere de Cassis over a mile on his next start.

Opposite top

SAINT-CLOUD, 23 March 2007

Hurricane Fly wins the Listed Prix Omnium II under Francois-Xavier Bertras in testing ground from subsequent Champion Stakes winner Literato and Spirit One. Jean-Luc Pelletan missed his race, but owner Hans-Peter Breitenstein said he was glad he made it over from a snowbound Switzerland. 'I just can't stop dreaming about Hurricane Fly, who we believe to be an extremely good horse. I'm sure people will try and buy him now but he's not for sale at the moment,' he said.

Opposite bottom

CHANTILLY, 9 May 2007

Hurricane Fly (second left) finishes fourth in the Group 3 Prix de Guiche behind Lawman, who was successful in the Prix du Jockey Club on his next start, Holocene (white cap) and Chinese Whisper (dark blue silks).

PUNCHESTOWN, 7 May 2008

After two more starts in France, Hurricane Fly was bought by George Creighton and sent to Willie Mullins in Ireland. He makes his Irish debut in a maiden hurdle at the Punchestown Festival and dismisses his 21 rivals with the minimum of fuss. He quickened to the front under Ruby Walsh after the second-last flight and had the race won in a few strides as he scored by 12 lengths from Afasheen.

AUTEUIL, 25 May 2008

Above Hurricane Fly and a delighted Ruby Walsh walk back to the winner's enclosure after their victory in the Gras Savoye Prix de Longchamp.

Below Hurricane Fly pictured in the winner's circle with his delighted connections after the Gras Savoye Prix de Longchamp.

AUTEUIL, 22 June 2008

Hurricane Fly (Davy Condon, centre) this time finishes second to Grivette in the Grade 1 Prix Alain du Breil, with stablemate and subsequent six-time Cheltenham Festival heroine Quevega in third. Hurricane Fly went on to have just one more start in France, the final race of his illustrious career in June 2015.

THE FIGURES tell the story. Everyone now knows that Hurricane Fly became one of the most enduring stars in racing history with a world record 22 wins at the highest level in an eight-season, 32-race jumping career. But back at the beginning of the 2008-9 season he was a light framed four-year-old who had already run ten times on the Flat and three times over hurdles and in normal circumstances this would become the busiest part of his career.

But Hurricane Fly was no normal horse and, every bit as important, Willie Mullins no ordinary trainer. In these first two full Irish seasons, Hurricane Fly ran just five times. True he won four of them and established himself as a future star but never doubt that in less patient hands the horse would have been just another talent added to the list of 'might have beens'.

Previous spread

LEOPARDSTOWN, 27 December 2008

Hurricane Fly and Paul Townend (blue) clear the final flight with Go Native in the paddypower.com Future Champion Novice Hurdle over two miles before going on to score by ten lengths. Willie Mullins said afterwards: 'That was certainly a very impressive performance. He's a horse who has everything: speed and stamina, which he showed over two and a half miles in France.'

FAIRYHOUSE, 30 November 2008

Hurricane Fly and Paul Townend jump the final flight in the
Bar One Racing Royal Bond Novice Hurdle from Donnas
Palm (centre) and Cousin Vinny (far side) for the first Grade 1
victory of his career.

PUNCHESTOWN, 28 April 2009

Hurricane Fly makes it three out of three for the season with a seven-length victory over Kempes (right) in the Evening Herald Champion Novice Hurdle at the Punchestown festival.

CLOSUTTON, 15 October 2009

Willie Mullins watches on as Hurricane Fly and Paul Townend set off for the gallops as preparations step up for the new season.

PUNCHESTOWN, 15 November 2009

Hurricane Fly (right) suffers his first defeat in
Ireland as he finishes third behind Solwhit (centre)
and Muirhead on his seasonal return in the
Dobbins & Madigans at Punchestown Hurdle.

HURRICANE FLY

PUNCHESTOWN, 23 April 2010

After missing the Cheltenham Festival with injury,
Hurricane Fly reappears at the Punchestown
festival. He renews rivalry with Solwhit and,
after jumping the final flight of the Rabobank
Champion Hurdle in second place (opposite top),
he fights back (opposite bottom) and draws level
(below) before taking the Grade 1 by a neck.

PUNCHESTOWN, 23 April 2010

Above Paul Townend gives a thumbs up after
Hurricane Fly's gutsy victory.

Opposite Lewis Creighton (left), grandson of part-
owner George, hugs Paul Townend in the winner's
enclosure with part-owner Frank Boyd looking on

BUT IT was worth the wait. An unforgettable, unbeaten five-race sequence, including the Champion Hurdles at both Cheltenham and Leopardstown, was some payback for the seasons gone before. Little wonder that Willie Mullins reflected wistfully 'I would have loved to have had him here' as he reflected on what his legendary father Paddy Mullins would have made of Hurricane Fly's Cheltenham glory saying: 'The preparation of this horse would have been half down to him. I imagined what he would have done in the same situation and tried to follow that.'

The Mullins family had already made a major mark in history. Hurricane Fly had many pages still to come.

Previous spread

CHELTENHAM, 15 March 2011

Ruby Walsh celebrates a first Stan James Champion Hurdle success on Hurricane Fly as the pair finish a length and a quarter clear of Peddlers Cross. Referring to the injury which ruled his star hurdler out of Cheltenham 12 months earlier, trainer Willie Mullins said: 'We've had an absolutely free run and I was pinching myself that everything was going right. We didn't have one day's setback.'

FAIRYHOUSE, 15 December 2010

Although he went through the top of the final flight in the Bar One Racing Hatton's Grace Hurdle on his reappearance he got the better of old rival and even-money favourite Solwhit by a length and a half.

Above

FAIRYHOUSE, 15 December 2010

Paul Townend gives Hurricane Fly a victory pat as they return to the winner's enclosure.

Opposite

LEOPARDSTOWN, 29 December 2010

Solwhit is again the victim as Hurricane Fly and Paul Townend roar to another Grade 1 success in the paddypower.com iPhone App Festival Hurdle at the Christmas meeting.

LEOPARDSTOWN, 23 January 2011

Above Photographers get their shots of Hurricane Fly, Paul Townend and Gail Carlisle in the winner's enclosure after the Irish Champion Hurdle.

Opposite top Gail Carlisle with Hurricane Fly before his first run in the BHP Insurances Irish Champion Hurdle.

Opposite bottom Hurricane Fly and Paul Townend again get the better of Solwhit, this time by three and a half lengths.

LEOPARDSTOWN, 23 January 2011		
BHP Insurances Irish Champion Hurdle		2m
1 Hurricane Fly	4/9F	P Townend
2 Solwhit	3/1	D Russell
3 Thousand Stars	14/1	Ms K Walsh
5 ran 3 1/2l, 2l		

RACING POST ANALYSIS: He seems to have everything one would hope to see in a potential champion hurdler.

CHELTENHAM, 13 March 2011

Hurricane Fly and workrider Aaron Madden on the gallops two days before his first attempt at the Champion Hurdle.

HURRICANE FLY

CHELTENHAM, 14 March 2011

Above Steam rises from Hurricane Fly as he and his stablemates continue their preparations for the festival.

Left Ruby Walsh, who only returned from a broken leg nine days earlier, casts an admiring glance at Hurricane Fly on the gallops.

CHELTENHAM, 15 March 2011

Stan James Champion Hurdle Challenge Trophy 2m1/2f

1	Hurricane Fly	11/4F	R Walsh
2	Peddlers Cross	9/2	J Maguire
3	Oscar Whisky	7/1	B Geraghty

11 ran 1 1/4l, 5l

RACING POST ANALYSIS: This brilliant display rids any previous doubts about his worth in beating the same horses all the time in Ireland, and it must be remembered that the horse so often second to him at home, Solwhit, is himself a six-time Grade 1 winner.

CHELTENHAM, 15 March 2011

Above Hurricane Fly (second left) and Peddlers Cross (left) clear the final flight in the Champion Hurdle.

Opposite top Ruby Walsh (right) drives Hurricane Fly to a length-and-a-quarter victory over Jason Maguire and Peddlers Cross.

Opposite bottom Ruby Walsh shows how much victory in the hurdling crown on Hurricane Fly means to him.

Left

CHELTENHAM, 15 March 2011

Eye of a superstar: Hurricane Fly after his
Champion Hurdle victory.

Below

FAIRYHOUSE, 24 April 2011

Hurricane Fly is paraded at the Irish Grand
National meeting following his first Champion
Hurdle triumph.

HURRICANE FLY

PUNCHESTOWN, 6 MAY 2011

Left Hurricane Fly crowns a magnificent season with a five-length victory over stablemate Thousand Stars (red cap, partly obscured) and Binocular (white cap) in the Rabobank Champion Hurdle at the Punchestown festival. Willie Mullins said afterwards: 'He was just awesome. I was a bit worried down the back but Ruby tells me he was never anxious. Hurricane Fly is not the biggest horse in the world but he has been so strong this season.'

PUNCHESTOWN, 6 MAY 2011

Top Ruby Walsh punches the air as he makes his way to the winner's enclosure.

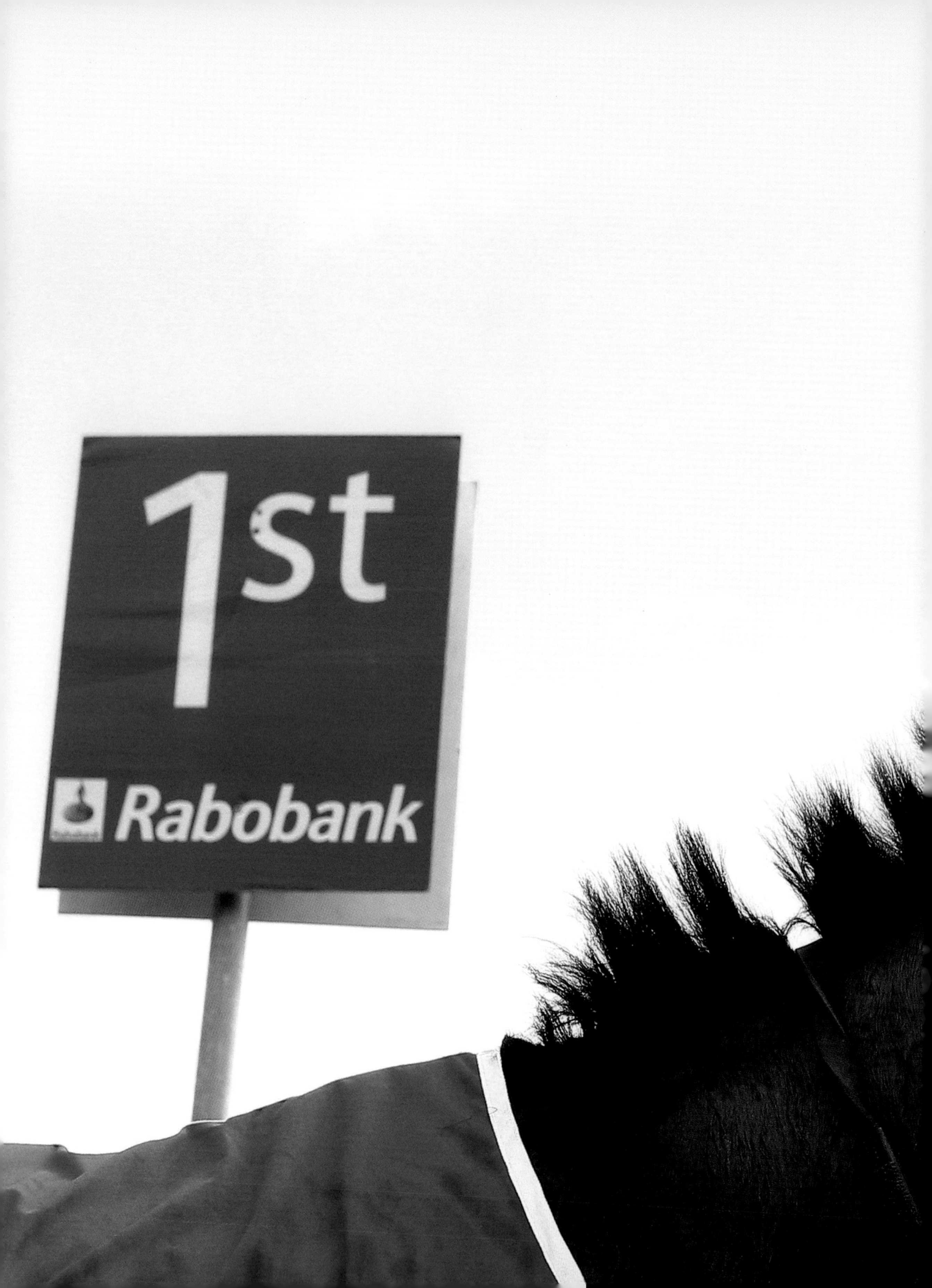
1st
Rabobank

OLD truths will always out. It's tough enough to win a title, even tougher to defend it. Hurricane Fly kept his Irish Champion crown but had to take defeat on the chin at Cheltenham. Never a big or a powerfully framed horse, many of us thought we had already seen the best of him.

What we had not yet fully recognised was the warrior's heart behind the talent. How lucky we would be that there were fully fifteen more battles yet to come.

Previous spread

PUNCHESTOWN, 27 April 2012

Number one: Hurricane Fly in the winner's enclosure after a two-and-a-half-length victory in the Rabobank Champion Hurdle at the spring festival. It was also a fifth win at the course and rounded off another successful season. It wasn't an altogether smooth ride for Ruby Walsh, who said afterwards: 'I'd say he wasn't right today. Horses who run as flat as he did today don't win unless they're exceptional. With a summer's grass to freshen him up, he'll be the horse we saw last year.'

LEOPARDSTOWN, 28 December 2011

Willie Mullins tells the media that Hurricane Fly
will not run in the December Festival Hurdle at the
Christmas meeting because he is not 100 per cent
happy with his stable star.

LEOPARDSTOWN, 28 January 2012

Giovanni Caiani, the breeder of Hurricane Fly, with his wife Raffaella (left) and daughter Martina, at the Irish Champion Hurdle meeting.

LEOPARDSTOWN, 29 January 2012			
BHP Insurance Irish Champion Hurdle			2m
1 Hurricane Fly	4/5F	R Walsh	
2 Oscars Well	8/1	R Power	
3 Thousand Stars	11/2	P Townend	
5 ran 6 1/2l, 3 1/2l			

RACING POST ANALYSIS: This was a thoroughly genuine performance, confirming him as probably the best hurdler since Istabraq.

LEOPARDSTOWN, 29 January 2012

Opposite top Hurricane Fly puts in a mighty leap at the first flight in the BHP Insurance Irish Champion Hurdle before putting in another superlative performance to beat Oscars Well by six and a half lengths. Willie Mullins said: 'That might have been Hurricane Fly's best-ever performance. I was surprised at how fit he appeared to be and to win the way he did completely surprised me.'

Opposite bottom Ruby Walsh debriefs Willie Mullins in the winner's enclosure after the Irish Champion Hurdle as photographers take their pictures.

CLOSUTTON, 21 February 2012

Willie Mullins at home with Hurricane Fly three
weeks before his stable star attempts to defend his
Champion Hurdle crown at Cheltenham.

CHELTENHAM, 13 March 2012

Hurricane Fly (second right) was sent off the 4-6 favourite for the Stan James Champion Hurdle but could finish only third behind Rock On Ruby (left) and Overturn (second left). He could not find the pace to launch a serious challenge under Ruby Walsh. Willie Mullins said afterwards: 'Ruby said when he asked him to get into the race coming down the hill the horse didn't find. He quickened to get a position before the last but he couldn't do any more and that was it.'

CHELTENHAM, 13 March 2012		
Stan James Champion Hurdle Challenge Trophy		2m1/2f
1 Rock On Ruby	11/1	N Fehily
2 Overturn	20/1	J Maguire
3 Hurricane Fly	4/6F	R Walsh
10 ran 3 3/4l, 1 3/4l		

RACING POST ANALYSIS: Ruby Walsh settled him out the back and made his move when angling out near the third-last, but it was apparent soon after he was in trouble and the first pair got away from him.

HURRICANE FLY

Hurricane Fly and Ruby Walsh returned to winning ways in the Rabobank Champion Hurdle as the pair led home a stable 1-2-3, with Zaidpour and Thousand Stars filling the places. Willie Mullins said: 'I wasn't impressed with him going to post first time and I'd say his class won him the race.'

WHO says that revenge is best served cold? Hurricane Fly's unbeaten journey to grab back his hurdle crown will always remain one of the most heart-warming of Cheltenham stories. As we look at these pictures all over again, we remember quite how life affirming days these were.

Even the English were getting used to him. He was never going to be a spectacular hero and his lack of exposure to English eyes had seen him consistently underrated. But now there was no denying the hero's role.

Previous spread

CHELTENHAM, 12 March 2013

A triumphant Ruby Walsh returns to the winner's enclosure after Hurricane Fly became the first horse since Comedy Of Errors in 1975 to regain the Champion Hurdle crown. It was the fourth of five successive victories during the season and the winning rider said afterwards: 'What he has along with all the class is an unbelievably big heart for a small horse, he is as tough as nails. He has never been short of stamina or guts and he jumped the last when I needed one today and ground it out to the line. He's a cracking horse and I'm pleased I got it back because he is a true champion hurdler.'

PUNCHESTOWN, 18 November, 2012

Right Ruby Walsh is a picture of concentration before Hurricane Fly makes his seasonal return in the Dobbins & Madigans @ Punchestown Morgiana Hurdle.

Below Hurricane Fly jumps the final flight of the Morgiana Hurdle ahead of Go Native, who falls, and he is left clear of Captain Cee Bee to record a 12-length victory. Willie Mullins said afterwards: 'We were just a bit worried today with him being fresh and running against two horses that were race fit, but he settled well in front, it worked well and we wouldn't be afraid to do that with him again. As he grows older he's getting more relaxed and easier to ride.'

HURRICANE FLY

LEOPARDSTOWN, 29 December 2012

Above Hurricane Fly and Ruby Walsh clear the final flight in the Istabraq Festival Hurdle on their way to a seven-length victory over Unaccompanied. 'He could have done no more. He got a lead, sat in behind Thousand Stars and quickened up nicely when he had to,' Willie Mullins said.

Opposite Ruby Walsh and Willie Mullins in the weighing room before the Istabraq Festival Hurdle.

LEOPARDSTOWN, 27 January 2013

Above Hurricane Fly parades in wintry conditions before the BHP Insurance Irish Champion Hurdle.

Right Hurricane Fly strolls to a five-length victory in the Irish Champion Hurdle from Thousand Stars (centre) and Binocular. Willie Mullins said afterwards: 'He was very good and is right back to his very best. He took off turning into the straight as if he'd just jumped into the race.' Jockey Ruby Walsh added: 'The Hurricane was very good today and I was very impressed. He did everything right and won as he liked.'

LEOPARDSTOWN, 27 January 2013

Tony McCoy, Paul Townend and Ruby Walsh could be forgiven if they were really talking about the weather rather than Hurricane Fly's Irish Champion Hurdle victory over Thousand Stars and Binocular.

Opposite top In the winner's enclosure after the Irish Champion Hurdle.

Opposite bottom Posing for the cameras.

LEOPARDSTOWN, 27 January 2013		
BHP Insurance Irish Champion Hurdle		2m
1 Hurricane Fly	1/6F	R Walsh
2 Thousand Stars	9/1	P Townend
3 Binocular	11/2	A P McCoy
5 ran 5l, nose		

RACING POST ANALYSIS: He did not have to come off the bridle to confirm he remains by far the best two-mile hurdler in Ireland.

CHELTENHAM, 10 March 2013

Above Hurricane Fly and Paul Townend on the gallops with Cleeve Hill offering a beautiful backdrop.

Right Hurricane Fly and Paul Townend (third left, blue hat) follow Quevega and Ruby Walsh (left) onto the gallops.

HURRICANE FLY

CHELTENHAM, 12 March 2013

Above Hurricane Fly and his jubilant connections in the winner's enclosure after the Champion Hurdle.

Opposite top left Hurricane Fly and Ruby Walsh are led out before the Champion Hurdle by Jack Madden and Gail Carlisle.

Opposite top right Hurricane Fly receives a well-deserved pat on the neck from Ruby Walsh after their Champion Hurdle success.

Opposite bottom Hurricane Fly clears the final flight in the Champion Hurdle from the previous year's winner Rock On Ruby (right), Countrywide Flame (second left) and Zarkandar. Willie Mullins said afterwards: 'This means a great deal. He's been posting these good performances all year. He's been doing it at home and doing it on the racetrack.'

CHELTENHAM, 12 March 2013		
Stan James Champion Hurdle Challenge Trophy		2m1/2f
1 Hurricane Fly	13/8F	R Walsh
2 Rock On Ruby	11/2	N Fehily
3 Countrywide Flame	16/1	D O'Regan
9 ran 2 1/2l, 1 3/4l		

RACING POST ANALYSIS: Despite now being a dual winner of the race, this track and quicker ground don't bring out the absolute best in him, so it was another imperious display from the champion.

CHELTENHAM, 12 March 2013

Top Gary Davies gives Hurricane Fly a well-deserved drink after the Champion Hurdle.

Above Willie Mullins talks to the press after Hurricane Fly's second Champion Hurdle victory.

PUNCHESTOWN, 26 April 2013

Hurricane Fly runs out a wide-margin winner of the Rabobank Champion Hurdle at the spring festival. He beats stablemate Thousand Stars (grey) by seven lengths with Rock On Ruby (left) a length further back in third. Willie Mullins said: 'The home work he did before this was probably as good as we've seen from him.'

Previous spread

PUNCHESTOWN, 26 April 2013

Hurricane Fly and Ruby Walsh win the Rabobank Champion Hurdle without being extended.

PUNCHESTOWN, 26 April 2013

Below Ruby is congratulated by racegoers as he heads back to the weighing room after the Rabobank Champion Hurdle.

Bottom Racegoers take photos of their hero.

PUNCHESTOWN, 26 April 2013

Above Ruby Walsh and Willie Mullins receive the trophy from Taoiseach Enda Kenny.

Right Ruby Walsh is interviewed after the Rabobank Champion Hurdle.

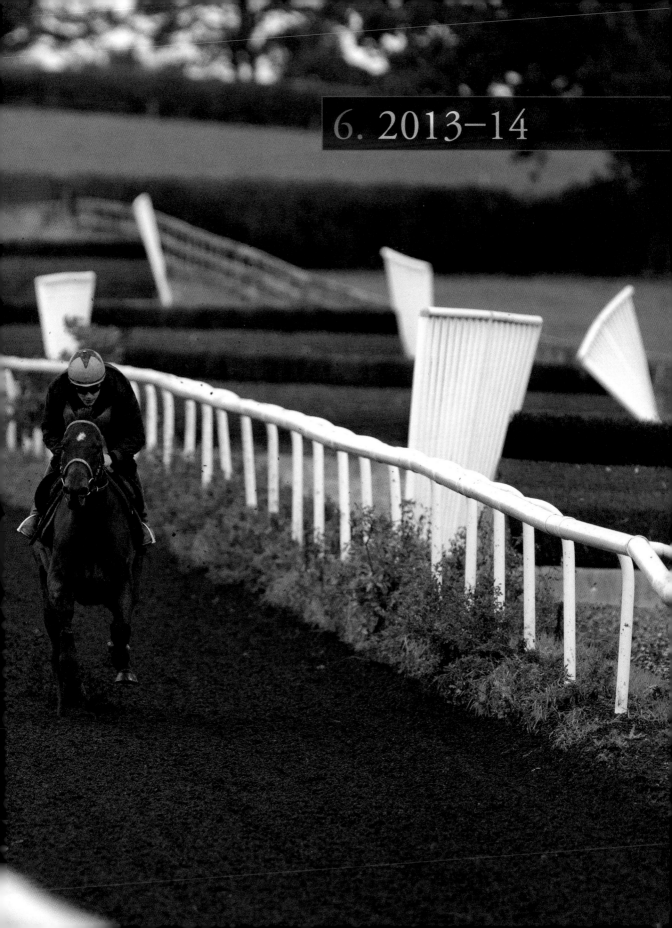

IT WAS never going to get any easier. At ten years old Hurricane
Fly was already the old wolf in the pack and the likes of Jezki and
Our Conor, four and five years his junior, were the young bloods
determined to beat him to the kill.

Twice he put both of them in their place at Leopardstown having first
set a new record of his own. But come Cheltenham he had to bow to
Jezki's power while poor Our Conor fell and paid the final forfeit fee.
Jezki was still master at Punchestown's end-of-season showdown.
Who would have thought that the old wolf was not finished yet?

Previous spread

CLOSUTTON, 26 October 2013

Hurricane Fly and Paul Townend work on the
gallops in preparation for the new season.

PUNCHESTOWN, 17 November 2013

Hurricane Fly and Ruby Walsh canter to post
before the StanJames.com Morgiana Hurdle.

PUNCHESTOWN, 17 November 2013

Ruby Walsh raises his whip in celebration when
crossing the line in the Morgiana Hurdle.

HURRICANE FLY

PUNCHESTOWN, 17 November 2013

Right Ruby Walsh with a number 17 saddlecloth in recognition of Hurricane Fly's 17th Grade 1 victory, surpassing the mark set by steeplechasing great Kauto Star and American Flat racing legend John Henry. Willie Mullins said afterwards: 'I'm very pleased that Hurricane Fly has set a world record. It is once-in-a-lifetime stuff and something you never expect to achieve in your career. He has been a very special horse for us and a huge help to the yard.'

Below Ruby Walsh's face in reflection on the winner's trophy after the Morgiana Hurdle.

HURRICANE FLY

PUNCHESTOWN, 17 November 2013

Hurricane Fly lights up the gloom in the winner's enclosure after his record-breaking victory in the Morgiana Hurdle.

CURRAGH, 20 October 2013

Willie Mullins directs operations as his string, including Hurricane Fly (third left), prepare to work.

Following comments made by Channel 4 Racing's lead commentator Simon Holt and the *Racing Post's* Topspeed Dave Edwards after his record-breaking victory, Patrick Mullins felt compelled to write to the *Racing Post* in defence of Hurricane Fly. Edwards had written: 'Hurricane Fly took all the plaudits for winning his 17th Grade 1 at the weekend but ten of those have been in fields of less than six runners against more or less the same opposition.' While Holt remarked it was spurious to compare Hurricane Fly's achievement with Group 1 winners on the Flat and that many of his wins had come in uncompetitive contests.

Opposite is Mullins' letter which appeared in the *Post* on 1 December 2013:

I FEEL I have to respond to the comments of Simon Holt and Dave Edwards about Hurricane Fly (Weekender, November 20).

Simon says 'Fly' has won 'uncompetitive contests – 11 of them at odds-on – which barely deserved their lofty status', while Dave says he has done his winning 'in fields of six or less against the same opposition'.

Both are, I would suggest, wrong and their views are coloured by them not rating Irish races highly simply because they aren't run in England.

In his 'uncompetitive' and 'small field' races, Fly has beaten more than 20 Grade 1 winners, 12 of them Cheltenham Festival winners and 16 of them multiple Grade 1 winners. This group have won two Champion Hurdles, three Supreme Novices', two Triumphs, three Christmas Hurdles, three Fighting Fifths and four Aintree Hurdles among the 50 Grade 1s they have won altogether.

Fly also beat Literato (winner of Group 1 Champion Stakes) and Spirit One (winner of Grade 1 Arlington Million) into second and third in a Listed race in France.

It is also important to remember Hurricane Fly missed the 2009 Supreme Novices' and the 2010 Champion Hurdle, won by Go Native and Binocular. He has beaten both of them, while neither has beaten him. Add to this the four other possible Grade 1s he missed around this time and the three possible ones he missed in 2011-12, and he would seem unlucky not to have more than 17.

In 14 of his Grade 1 wins, the second horse has won two or more Grade 1s. Only twice has he had a non-Grade 1 winner finish second to him. Uncompetitive? A small field doesn't mean a bad race – it is harder to beat one good horse than ten average ones.

Being odds-on shows nothing other than you are going to be very hard to beat, as a champion should be. Frankel was odds-on in all of his Grade 1s. Black Caviar was regularly sent off 1-20. Istabraq was nearly always odds-on and I would imagine it is difficult to get odds against on Usain Bolt any time he lines up.

There seems to be a thing about him beating Solwhit (five times) and Thousand Stars (three times) into second. Frankel beat Excelebration four times, at odds-on every time without leaving his home soil, but that quite rightly does not take away from his amazing legacy. Exotic Dancer was placed five times behind Kauto Star, but again this doesn't take away from Kauto Star being one of the sport's greats.

Solwhit has won eight Grade 1 races, five in Ireland and three in England. He beat Punjabi into second at Punchestown after Punjabi had won the Champion Hurdle, with Quevega and Sizing Europe in third and fourth.

He also beat Sublimity into second at Leopardstown, another Champion Hurdle winner. I dare anyone to describe him as anything other than a genuine Grade 1 horse.

Thousand Stars has won a Grade 1 over two miles in Ireland, two Grade 1s over three miles in France and was twice only beaten a neck in a Grade 1 over two miles four in England. Indeed, he beat Binocular at Punchestown 2011 when second to Fly and beat Rock on Ruby at Punchestown 2013 when again second to Fly.

The last two British-trained Champion Hurdle winners couldn't beat Thousand Stars at Punchestown over two miles. He was also only a length off The New One in Aintree this year. He can only be described as a genuine Grade 1 horse too.

Hurricane Fly made these horses look ordinary and some have assumed they are. However, they have both won Grade 1s outside Ireland as well as in. When there is a champion the competition looks weak because one is so far ahead of the rest.

Hurricane Fly has defied history in regaining his title after losing it, he has broken a world record despite having three periods of missed time, he has beaten the best over hurdles for the past five years as well as Group 1 winners on the Flat and he is a champion. Show him the respect he deserves.

PATRICK MULLINS, County Carlow

LEOPARDSTOWN, 29 December 2013

Left Hurricane Fly jumps the last alongside Our Conor (right) before landing his 18th Grade 1 in the Ryanair Hurdle. For the first time since the 2010 Hatton's Grace Hurdle at Fairyhouse Hurricane Fly was allowed to go off odds-against in a race on Irish soil. Willie Mullins said afterwards: 'It was a good performance but I've seen him better.'

Below Ruby Walsh looks behind for non-existent dangers as Jezki (left) and Our Conor are left trailing in his wake in the Ryanair Hurdle.

Opposite Ruby Walsh acknowledges the crowd after Hurricane Fly's victory in the Ryanair Hurdle.

LEOPARDSTOWN, 29 December 2013

Above Winning connections celebrate Hurricane Fly's Ryanair Hurdle success.

Left Ruby and Gillian Walsh with daughters Elsa and Isabelle after the race.

LEOPARDSTOWN, 26 January 2014

Right Hurricane Fly parades before the BHP Insurance Irish Champion Hurdle.

Below Ruby looks relaxed on the Fly in the parade ring before the race.

LEOPARDSTOWN, 26 January 2014

Above Ruby Walsh punches the air as Hurricane Fly secures a fourth successive victory in the Irish Champion Hurdle. Hurricane Fly finished a length and a half clear of Our Conor. Willie Mullins admitted his relief that his stable star had delivered despite a foot scare in the lead-up to the race. 'I've always thought the world of this horse but he's gone up in my estimation. It was an extraordinary effort in the circumstances,' he said.

Opposite top Willie Mullins congratulates Ruby Walsh after the Fly's 19th top level success.

Opposite bottom Hurricane Fly enjoys a bucket of water after the Irish Champion Hurdle.

LEOPARDSTOWN, 26 January 2014			
BHP Insurance Irish Champion Hurdle			2m
1 Hurricane Fly	4/7F	R Walsh	
2 Our Conor	5/1	D Mullins	
3 Captain Cee Bee	50/1	M Walsh	
4 ran 1 1/2l, 1 1/4l			

RACING POST ANALYSIS: His performance was in some ways reminiscent of his Champion Hurdle win last season as he came off the bridle and maybe hit a slight flat spot between the last two hurdles, but you could only admire what he produced after the last.

CLOSUTTON, 19 February 2014

Left Paul Townend takes Hurricane Fly through a stream during a press morning ahead of the following month's Champion Hurdle.

Middle Hurricane Fly and Paul Townend (left) alongside Quevega and Jack Madden.

Bottom A worm's eye view of Hurricane Fly working on the gallops with Paul Townend in the saddle.

Previous spread

LEOPARDSTOWN, 26 January 2014

Hurricane Fly is congratulated by his adoring public around the winner's enclosure.

CHELTENHAM, 9 March 2014

Hurricane Fly and Gail Carlisle (left), alongside
Quevega and Jack Madden, take in the scene as
they prepare for the festival.

CHELTENHAM, 10 March 2014

Left Willie Mullins accompanies Hurricane Fly and Ruby Walsh onto the gallops.

Above Hurricane Fly enjoys a pick of grass with Ruby Walsh after stretching his legs on the gallops.

CHELTENHAM, 11 March 2014

Hurrcane Fly (third left) is among the leaders as they approach the second flight in the Stan James Champion Hurdle before he finished fourth behind Jezki, My Tent Or Yours and The New One. Willie Mullins said afterwards: 'I thought we were in good form coming into the race, so it's disappointing to be fourth, but maybe that's where we are now.'

CHELTENHAM, 11 March 2014		
Stan James Champion Hurdle Challenge Trophy		2m1/2f
1 Jezki	9/1	B Geraghty
2 My Tent Or Yours	3/1	A P McCoy
3 The New One	100/30	S Twiston-Davies
4 Hurricane Fly	11/4	F R Walsh
9 ran nk, 2 1/2l, 2 1/4l		

RACING POST ANALYSIS: Giving his all under pressure, the tank emptied from the final flight and he went out on his shield.

PUNCHESTOWN, 2 May, 2014

Opposite top Hurricane Fly leads the parade for the Racing Post Champion Hurdle followed by Jezki and Steps To Freedom.

Opposite bottom Jezki, the hero of the Champion Hurdle at Cheltenham, leads over the final flight from Hurricane Fly before going on to win by three and a quarter lengths. Willie Mullins said afterwards: 'I thought Jezki was travelling better than our fellow at all stages. I don't think we have any excuses. We came here hoping for the best but were beaten by the better horse.'

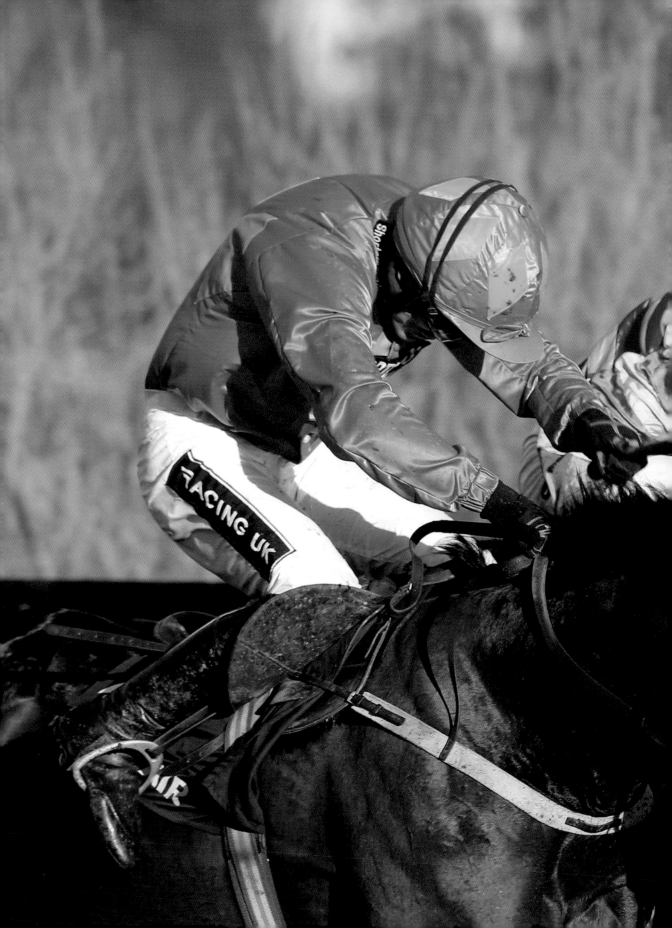

For champions the final days are always the hardest. Not for nothing did Patrick Mullins talk of the 'rage against the dying of the light.' Of course Hurricane Fly was not the horse he was but he was still a champion and how wonderfully he stated that when he twice put Jezki back in his box and then took the Irish title for that fifth consecutive time.

At Cheltenham, Punchestown and finally at Auteuil we knew we were seeing the last of him. But the exit was anything but pitiful. All careers have to come to closure and Hurricane Fly could be no different. But what a difference he had made. Hold on to these memories. It will not only be Patrick Mullins who will be wanting to tell the grandchildren on his knee.

Previous spread

LEOPARDSTOWN, 29 December, 2014

Hurricane Fly and Jezki fight out the finish to the Ryanair Hurdle at the Christmas meeting. They were separated by just half a length at the finish, after which Willie Mullins said: 'He's the best horse anyone has had over hurdles, and I would say I'll never have another like him. He's unique.'

PUNCHESTOWN, 16 November, 2014

Above Hurricane Fly (right) gains a small measure of revenge over Jezki with a two-and-a-quarter-length victory in the StanJames.com Morgiana Hurdle. It was a 20th win at the top level for Hurricane Fly and afterwards Willie Mullins said: 'He's getting older but if he can reproduce that sort of form you'd be hopeful of more to come from him in the top races.'

Right Hurricane Fly with his connections after the Morgiana Hurdle.

Bottom right Ruby Walsh and Willie Mullins in the winner's enclosure after the race.

CLOSUTTON, 17 December 2014

Above Paul Townend gets into the Christmas spirit when dressing up as Father Christmas for his morning ride.

Left Hurricane Fly is accompanied by Ballycasey (centre) and Champagne Fever (right) for his morning exercise.

LEOPARDSTOWN, 29 December 2014

Right Hurricane Fly (left) jumps the last alongside Jezki before outbattling his rival on the run-in to land the Ryanair Hurdle.

Below A jubilant Ruby Walsh after Fly's victory in the Ryanair Hurdle.

LEOPARDSTOWN, 25 January 2015

Above Ruby Walsh and Tony McCoy (right) walk out into the parade ring before the BHP Insurances Irish Champion Hurdle.

LEOPARDSTOWN, 29 December 2014

Opposite top Ruby Walsh is greeted by his wife Gillian after the Ryanair Hurdle.

Opposite middle Hurricane Fly and Ruby Walsh take in the applause from the festive crowd.

Opposite bottom Ruby is interviewed after Hurricane Fly's 21st Grade 1 victory.

LEOPARDSTOWN, 25 January 2015

BHP Insurances Irish Champion Hurdle 2m

1	Hurricane Fly	11/10F	R Walsh
2	Artic Fire	8/1	P Townend
3	Jezki	5/4	A P McCoy

6 ran 3 1/2l, 4l

RACING POST ANALYSIS: The value of this race as a Champion Hurdle trial will be revealed in the fullness of time, but it can't be denied that the winner is one of the true greats amongst two-mile hurdlers as he landed this race for the fifth time.

LEOPARDSTOWN, 25 January 2015

Hurricane Fly records what was to be his final victory – his 22nd at Grade 1 level and tenth in ten starts at Leopardstown – in the Irish Champion Hurdle. He finishes three and a half lengths clear of stablemate Arctic Fire, with Jezki four lengths further back in third. Willie Mullins said afterwards: 'It's hard to believe he's an 11-year-old and not five or six.'

HURRICANE FLY

LEOPARDSTOWN, 25 January 2015

Opposite Ruby Walsh gives Hurricane Fly a pat on the neck after the Irish Champion Hurdle.

Above Ruby Walsh celebrates a fifth successive Irish Champion Hurdle win for Hurricane Fly.

Right Ruby and the Fly canter past the stands in front of a rapturous Irish crowd.

HURRICANE FLY

LEOPARDSTOWN, 25 January 2015

Left Hurricane Fly returns to a tremendous ovation following the Irish Champion Hurdle, after which Ruby Walsh said: 'Apart from Cheltenham I've never heard a horse get a reception like that from a crowd anywhere.'

Top A beaming Ruby Walsh with Hurricane Fly in the winner's enclosure.

Above The smiling connections receive their trophies after the Fly's final victory.

CLOSUTTON, 23 February, 2015

In his box during a media morning ahead of the
Cheltenham Festival.

CHELTENHAM, 9 March 2015

Dawn breaks as Hurricane Fly works on the gallops before his final Champion Hurdle challenge.

Right Paul Townend checks his phone during a moment's break on Hurricane Fly, while Ruby Walsh on Annie Power looks on.

CHELTENHAM, 10 March 2015

Faugheen and Ruby Walsh win the Stan James Champion Hurdle for Willie Mullins, with Arctic Fire (Danny Mullins, purple) and Hurricane Fly (Paul Townend, second right) completing a one-two-three for the master of Closutton. The trainer said afterwards: 'Hurricane Fly ran a terrific race and I thought he was going to get right into it after the second last. Paul was very happy with how he ran. That was no disgrace.'

CHELTENHAM, 10 March 2015		
Stan James Champion Hurdle Challenge Trophy 2m1/2f		
1 Faugheen	4/5F	R Walsh
2 Arctic Fire	20/1	1 D Mullins
3 Hurricane Fly	8/1	P Townend
8 ran 1 1/2l, 5l		

RACING POST ANALYSIS: The ground was quick enough for him and he would have preferred more of a test.

PUNCHESTOWN, 30 April 2015

The sun begins to set on Hurricane Fly after he steps up to three miles and finishes second to Jezki in the Ladbrokes World Series Hurdle. Willie Mullins said afterwards: 'It was Jezki's day and fair play to him. Hurricane Fly wasn't as fluent as the winner at a couple of hurdles and that possibly made the difference.'

CURRAGH, 13 September 2015

Hurricane Fly finished sixth of 15 in the French Champion Hurdle in early June and at the end of the summer he was retired. He then took part in a Parade of Champions at the Curragh during Irish Champions Weekend. It was a fitting end to an illustrious career.

WHAT THEY SAID

WILLIE MULLINS, trainer

Hurricane Fly was a wonderful servant, a very special horse. His aggressive attitude to the job was one of his major assets. Every day he went out to race he wanted to win. And the precision of his jumping when it mattered, especially at the last hurdle in so many of his races, was another big part of his success story. He had the ideal combination of speed, stamina and courage.

His owners George Creighton, his son Andrew and grandson Lewis, and Rose and Frank Boyd, have been fantastic and they always gave me a free rein throughout Hurricane Fly's career.

Of all his big-race wins I suppose the first of his two Champion Hurdle victories at Cheltenham in 2011 was extra special. It was a race we really wanted to win and he hadn't made it to the festival as a novice in 2009 or when we hoped to run him in the Champion Hurdle in 2010.

Setting a world record for Grade 1 or Group 1 wins when winning the Morgiana Hurdle, his 17th top-level success, at Punchestown in November 2013 was another big day, while his record at Leopardstown was both perfect and amazing.

He ran at Leopardstown ten times and was never beaten there. All those wins were in Grade 1 races and we'll never forget the huge reception he got from the crowd there in January 2015 when he won the Irish Champion Hurdle for the fifth consecutive year.

Ruby Walsh was always a huge fan of the horse and had complete faith in him, while Paul Townend played a huge role in his career. He rode him in all his work and also won six races on him. Gail Carlisle looked after him and did a terrific job with a horse who means the world to her.

The Hurricane had a few training setbacks early in his career because of the type of horse he was – he always wanted to go at things hard on the gallops – and Paul did a great job minding him.

I've often been asked if I ever considered picking out a few Flat races to run him in. It did cross my mind some years back but I decided against it. I took the view that doing so would not have been conducive to getting him to settle for jumping hurdles. As it was, it took three to four years to get him to settle like a normal horse, and when he eventually learned to settle he settled almost too well at times.

People tend to remember a horse's more recent races rather than those from early in his career, and for that reason I suppose his rivalry with Jezki towards the end of his career will be recalled for many years to come.

RUBY WALSH, JOCKEY

There were days I'll never forget with Hurricane Fly. The reception he got from the crowd at Leopardstown in January 2015 was unreal. A bit like Kauto Star in Haydock and Kempton during a season when people thought he was gone, the crowd just warmed to him even more. And it was the same with the Fly. He was good at Punchestown for his last Morgiana triumph and good at Leopardstown at Christmas, but in the Irish Champion Hurdle he and Jezki went hammer and tongs and it was some atmosphere coming back in.

Some days are special for different reasons. When he won his first Champion Hurdle in 2011 I had been injured all winter and was worried about getting back on him, and when I did and when he won it was an amazing feeling, a huge day for me. In 2012 things just didn't go right for him and he had a point to prove in 2013 – I felt I had anyway. To regain his Champion Hurdle was sweet and proved to me he was the best hurdler I have ridden, without doubt.

While we have a few stars in the yard that have that potential, they have to prove themselves over many seasons to make that potential a reality and match Hurricane Fly for longevity.

I was very lucky to ride the horses I consider to be the greatest chaser and hurdler of their generation, Kauto Star and Hurricane Fly. They had everything: the ability and the longevity. They also had soundness of mind and limb.

Hurricane Fly's attitude separated him from the others. Even now at home he has that bit of swagger, that cockiness. You can have all the money in the world but you need a bit of luck to come across horses like these and I'm just eternally grateful that Willie came across that fellow while I was riding.

There'll be talk now about erecting statues and naming races after him, but as far as I am concerned I have all the best memories of him – looking out between his ears!

PAUL TOWNEND, jockey

He put me on the map, it's as simple as that. Without him I would never have got to where I am. When you look back on it now, to think that Hurricane Fly was my first ever ride in a Grade 1 when I was just 17, you'd ask yourself was Willie mad to let me up on him given how inexperienced I was? It was a real springboard for me.

We always thought he was a good horse but the day he beat Go Native at Leopardstown he really showed what he was made of. He was awesome that day. That experience, when he accelerated off the home turn, was definitely the best experience I've ever had on a horse.

His raw ability is obviously a big factor but his will to win was unbelievable. If you get stuck into him in a finish, he will always find for you. I remember riding him at Punchestown back in 2010 and he had every opportunity up the home straight to lie down and give in and no-one would have held it against him because he hadn't run since the previous November but he didn't want to accept defeat. You could almost feel him eye-balling Solwhit and wanting to get by him. He was one in a billion and I was one of the very lucky ones to have got to ride him.

GAIL CARLISLE, travelling head girl and Hurricane Fly's minder

I started looking after him before the 2010 season and since then he has taken priority over everything in my life. Fly got sorted before anything else was done if I was going racing – my life revolved around him. I would have to ride him, get him groomed and cleaned, out in his paddock and have all that done before I would go anywhere with any of the other horses.

If he was going racing or to parade somewhere, I didn't take a day off, even if I was supposed to have a free day. My holidays had to wait until Fly went on his holidays, I came back to work when he came back in. He was a little dude but his attitude helped to make him what he was. All the good ones have their own kinks and he definitely had his.

There had been so much talk over the last two seasons about him finishing that it was always in the back of my mind but it drifted way back when he came back into training and was so well.

It will be strange not to go racing with him but he is still here, and is out in the paddock enjoying himself.

11211/131/1111/1131/11111/1114/21113-26

HURRICANE FLY

WORLD RECORD
22 GRADE 1 WINS

KAUTO STAR
16 GRADE 1 WINS

JOHN HENRY

14 GRADE 1 WINS

ISTABRAQ

10/10 AT LEOPARDSTOWN including Irish Champion Hurdle five years in a row

OVERALL HURDLES RECORD 24/32

LONGEST WINNING SEQUENCE 9

In 32 starts over hurdles he was sent off longer than 3-1 on only occasion, when third behind stablemate Faugheen in the 2015 Champion Hurdle. His shortest-priced win was at 1-16 against four rivals in the 2013 Morgiana Hurdle at Punchestown

He appeared at only two Irish tracks other than Leopardstown, Fairyhouse (2-2) and Punchestown (9-12)

He finished out of the first three only twice in 32 runs over hurdles, when fourth in the 2014 Champion Hurdle and sixth at Auteuil on his final start

CAREER IN SUMMARY

2006

11 July	La Teste De Buch	good	Prix De Biganos	6	F-X Bertras		2ND	£1,793.10
2 Aug	Vichy	good	Prix Des Jouvenceaux Et Des Jouvencelles (Listed)	7	F Spanu		6TH	-
14 Aug	Clairefontaine	good	Prix Matahawk	7	F-X Bertras	6/1	2ND	£2,620.69
10 Sept	Longchamp	good	Prix Du Casino De Cassis	8	F-X Bertras		3RD	£1,966.00

2007

4 March	Mont-de-marsan	very soft	Prix Achille Fould	7	F-X Bertras	87/10	WON	£4,054.05
23 March	Saint-Cloud	good	Prix Omnium II (Listed)	8	F-X Bertras	12/1	WON	£17,568
15 April	Longchamp	good to soft	Prix De Fontainbleu (Gp3)	7	F-X Bertras	53/10	8TH	-
9 May	Chantilly	soft	Prix De Guiche (Gp3)	9	F-X Bertras	15/1	4TH	£5,405
25 June	Longchamp	good to soft	Prix Daphnis (Gp3)	9	F-X Bertras		7TH	-
28 July	Maisons-Laffitte		Prix Eugene Adam (Gp2)	10	J Victoire		7TH	-

2007-08

7 May	Punchestown	good to firm	www.Punchestown.com Maiden Hurdle	16	R Walsh	9/10F	WON	£6,097.06

2008-09

25 May	Auteuil	very soft	Gras Savoye Prix De Logchamp Hurdle (Gd3)	19.5	R Walsh	21/10	WON	£43,015
22 June	Auteuil	very soft	Prix Alain Du Breil Hurdle (Gd1)	19.5	D Condon	17/10	2ND	£89,338
30 Nov	Fairyhouse	soft	Bar One Racing Royal Bond Novice Hurdle (Gd1)	16	P Townend	2/1F	WON	£43,014.71
27 Dec	Leopardstown	yielding to soft	PaddyPower.com Future Champion Novice Hurdle (Gd1)	16	P Townend	EvsF	WON	£38,235.29
28 April	Punchestown	soft	Evening Herald Champion Novice Hurdle (Gd1)	16	R Walsh	4/6F	WON	£60,194.17

2009-10

15 Nov	Punchestown	heavy	Dobbins & Madigans At Punchestown Hurdle (Gd1)	16	P Townend	8/13F	3RD	£7,427.18
23 April	Punchestown	good	Rabobank Champion Hurdle (Gd1)	16	P Townend	3/1	WON	£90,265.49

2010-11

15 Dec	Fairyhouse	soft	Bar One Racing Hatton's Grace Hurdle (Gd1)	20	P Townend	11/4	WON	£48,893.81
29 Dec	Leopardstown	heavy	PaddyPower.com Iphone App Festival Hurdle (Gd1)	16	P Townend	8/11F	WON	£51,769.91

23 Jan	Leopardstown	soft	BHP Insurances Irish Champion Hurdle (Gd1)	16	P Townend	4/9F	WON	£61,637.93
15 March	Cheltenham	good	Stan James Champion Hurdle Challenge Trophy (Gd1)	16.5	R Walsh	11/4F	WON	£210,937
6 May	Punchestown	good	Rabobank Champion Hurdle (Gd1)	16	R Walsh	1/2F	WON	£82,758.62

2011-12

29 Jan	Leopardstown	heavy	BHP Insurance Irish Champion Hurdle (Gd1)	16	R Walsh	4/5F	WON	£59,583.33
13 March	Cheltenham	good	Stan James Champion Hurdle Challenge Trophy (Gd1)	16.5	R Walsh	4/6F	3RD	£210,715.00
27 April	Punchestown	heavy	Rabobank Champion Hurdle (Gd1)	16	R Walsh	4/11F	WON	£80,000

2012-13

18 Nov	Punchestown	heavy	Dobbins & Madigans @ Punchestown Morgiana Hurdle (Gd1)	16	R Walsh	2/5F	WON	£40,000
29 Dec	Leopardstown	soft	Istabraq Festival Hurdle (Gd1)	16	R Walsh	1/5F	WON	£46,041.67
27 Jan	Leopardstown	soft to heavy	BHP Insurance Irish Champion Hurdle (Gd1)	16	R Walsh	1/6F	WON	£58,130.08
12 March	Cheltenham	soft	Stan James Champion Hurdle Challenge Trophy (Gd1)	16.5	R Walsh	13/8F	WON	£227,800
26 April	Punchestown	heavy	Rabobank Champion Hurdle (Gd1)	16	R Walsh	1/4F	WON	£97,154.47

2013-14

17 Nov	Punchestown	yielding	StanJames.com Morgiana Hurdle (Gd1)	16	R Walsh	1/16F	WON	£39,024.39
29 Dec	Leopardstown	soft	Ryanair Hurdle (Gd1)	16	R Walsh	11/10F	WON	£48,780.49
26 Jan	Leopardstown	soft to heavy	BHP Insurance Irish Champion Hurdle (Gd1)	16	R Walsh	4/7F	WON	£59,583.33
11 March	Cheltenham	good to soft	Stan James Champion Hurdle Challenge Trophy (Gd1)	16.5	R Walsh	11/4F	4TH	£22,279.40
2 May	Punchestown	good to yielding	Racing Post Champion Hurdle (Gd1)	16	R Walsh	Evs	2ND	£31,666.67

2014-15

16 Nov	Punchestown	soft	StanJames.com Morgiana Hurdle (Gd1)	16	R Walsh	15/8	WON	£40,000
29 Dec	Leopardstown	soft	Ryanair Hurdle (Gd1)	16	R Walsh	5/6F	WON	£50,000
25 Jan	Leopardstown	yielding	BHP Insurance Irish Champion Hurdle (Gd1)	16	R Walsh	11/10F	WON	£51,162.79
10 March	Cheltenham	good to soft	Stan James Champion Hurdle Challenge Trophy (Gd1)	16.5	P Townend	4/5F	3RD	£42,800.00
30 April	Punchestown	yielding	Ladbrokes World Series Hurdle (Gd1)	24	R Walsh	6/4F	2ND	£29,457.36
7 June	Auteuil	very soft	Grande Course De Haies D'Auteuil (Gd1)	25.5	R Walsh	6/4F	6TH	£10,038.76